AF414973

Dedication

*This book is called **EYES WIDE OPEN** for a reason. Scales will be removed from your eyes, in the name of Jesus. My prayer for readers who have lost their sight. I pray God will remove the veil over your eyes. I pray that this book will allow you to increase your faith to fully trust in the Lord when your eyes cannot see. I pray for fresh insight and vision again. It's time to see yourself the way God sees you. This time I insist that you look again, with your **EYES WIDE OPEN.***

ACKNOWLEDGMENTS

To my family, friends, my support system I love you all dearly. Thank you for your prayers, your thoughts and words of advice as I continue this journal and navigate my walk with Christ. Thank you all for truly seeing me and having the capacity to hold space for me in areas where I am growing. Thank you for listening. I SEE you, and you SEE me.

Table of Contents

Chapter 1

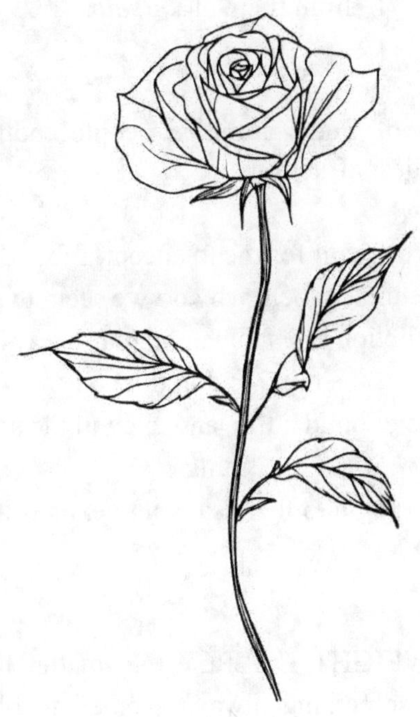

1

AFFLICTIONS

"Many are the afflictions of the
righteous, but the LORD delivers him
from them all." *Psalm 34:19*

*M*any of God's anointed people endure the
hardest afflictions.

This truth was difficult for me to accept. I found myself asking
God, If you love us so much, why do we seem to suffer the most?
Affliction can show up in many ways: in
the mind and in the body,
in our attempts to build a life, and even in the small, everyday
things
that begin to feel heavy and exhausting.

I FELT THIS WEIGHT DEEPLY. No matter how hard I tried
to push forward, something always seemed to block my
progress. I would start things but struggle to finish them. At
times, I felt as though something unseen was hindering me from
moving further. Discouragement crept in, and I found myself
wanting to give up.
This kind of struggle is frustrating for any believer. Yet, we
cannot grow weary, and we cannot quit. That is exactly what the
enemy desires, but we must resist the urge to stop. As I began
studying the word affliction, I thought surely God would not cause
delays, because He said in His Word that, "no good thing will be
withheld from them that walk uprightly" (Psalm 84:11).

Still, while reading the book of Samuel, the Lord led me to the story of Hannah. I had read Hannah's story many times, how she prayed and asked the Lord for a child, but tis time, I noticed something different.

The Scripture says the Lord shut up her womb *(1 Samuel 1:6)*. This was shocking to me. I thought, wow, so God can allow things to be blocked as well.

AS I CONTINUED READING, I noticed how Hannah's heart posture changed. Even in her barrenness, she chose to worship and cast her cares onto the Lord. She surrendered her desire to give birth and placed the matter fully into God's hands. It wasn't until she gave God total surrender and control that things shifted. The Lord wanted Hannah's devotion and her first fruits. Not only did she surrender her desire for a child, but she also made a vow. She promised that if God gave her a son, she would offer him back to the Lord for His use. Samuel was the promise the Lord gave to her, and in return, Hannah honored God by giving her son back to Him. This reminds me of the scripture that says, *"Honor the LORD with your wealth and with the first fruits of all your crops" (Proverbs 3:9)*. This is exactly what Hannah did, and in return, the Lord opened her womb. I say all of this to say: even though the Lord shut up Hannah's womb and she was afflicted, she still pressed her way toward God. She surrendered to His plans and His way. Maybe we can take something from Hannah's story. Instead of trying to avoid the issue, surrender that pain, problem, or thing that has been taunting you to the Lord. Offer up a sacrifice that will be pleasing to Him.

HE WILL HANDLE THE REST.

AS YOU READ, allow yourself to sit with the weight of affliction without trying to explain it away. Affliction is not a sign of failure or abandonment; it is often the place where God begins to open our eyes. Some parts of this chapter may feel heavy, unfamiliar, or uncomfortable. Let them meet you where you are.

Pause when each poem resonates with you. Pay attention to the moments that stir emotion or raise questions. Do not push those feelings aside. This chapter invites you to acknowledge pain we deal with around waiting, love, and frustrations.
As you read, my prayer is that you see clearly. What God reveals here is not meant to burden you, but to prepare you.

Read with humility.
Read with openness.
Read with your EYES WIDE OPEN.

C onstant Weight

Constant fight, constant struggle, the weight of waiting on
God to move and to hold out is tiresome, no I'm not
bugging. Constant weight to stay seen, and stay current
on social media. Everyday normalcy turns into usage for
content just for you to feel relevant.
Constant battles, constant setbacks, and unfortunately
constant disappointments.
The constant weight of the world thinking what you do is
not enough, it's not sufficient. How do you cope? How
do you learn to let go so you can heal?
From the constant weight on your shoulders, maybe send
up a prayer to God and this time, keep it real.
Be specific with your prayers and what's on your heart,
say what's on your mind, please take your time. No rush.
Apply pressure, be persistent and relentless in your
prayer. This constant weight that's on your back is only
holding you up, keeping you down, and simply just a
waste of time.

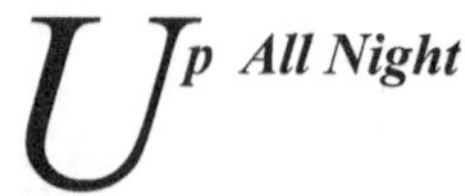

*U*p *All Night*

THOUGHTS ARE FLOODING my mind about what I'm gonna do.

Am I making the right decision? And if I could see it through. My thoughts keep me up sometimes late at night. My dreams, my goals, my family, even my love life. Everyday I'm praying like Lord is this right? "What are you saying to me," says my heart. Take away these anxious thoughts. Anxiety and depression, you have no place here. These thoughts feel my mind, but then I begin to pray, and God reminds me as he said in his word, the steps of a good man are ordered. Trust me, it's gonna be alright.

*H*alf As Bad

Never discount what you have to
offer like it's not a good idea.

Psyching yourself up,
saying your work is not half as bad.

Understand that comparisons will
rob you of your joy.

You must see that the people that's
assigned to you
will stay around
simply cause it's you.

So, don't panic,
or paint this image in your mind
that what you have to offer this
world
is not good enough.

Like who we are,
what we do, or
create
is basic stuff.

Sleeping on your dreams and
talents, telling everyone
you're not half as bad.

Discounting your services,

thinking it's not good
enough.

Take courage and
be of good heart,
you are more than enough.

Believe you can.

It's a process,

so go with the flow,
Don't rush it.

You could be sitting
on the next greatest
invention.

You never know
until you try.

Body Talk

MY MIND TELLS ME NO, but my body says otherwise .

Why stay with this man?
He shows no effort,
No emotions,
or space to properly hold you.
But you stay and pretend as if there is more. Can't
you see what he's already showing you?

TIME WASTED, you get yourself naked and aroused because that's the only way you can have him to satisfy your thirst for affection, dreams and intellectual conversations. Yet you're still EMPTY. Time is steady wasting, and you stay because he fills a void in your heart that says, "what if this is only as good as it gets?" So, you stay and settle. You open yourself up to let him in with hopes that he will come in you. He wastes his seeds instead, as if who you are is not worthy enough to be the woman to carry his child. Yet, you still stayed and accepted it. Didn't you know that what's in you is the birth of a nation? So why do you settle? You have allowed your body to rule and rain over you for far too long. Settling for breadcrumbs, minimum effect, just to get you to stay. This right here is not befitting of you. There is a generation WAITING ON YOU that can only be birth through YOUR faith. This is why you must wait. I thought you said, "you loved me". Believe and have faith in me, your God who has never forgotten you.

So, tell me why do you use your body as if it's nothing? Like there is no value or substance. I SEE what you haven't realized and only pray that the man you choose will see you first. You tell me things like, "the heart wants what the heart wants." Have you ever considered wanting me?

In all honesty and truth, your heart was still hurting. And yes, I know that you have been searching. Maybe that's why you couldn't put me first. Seek me and the kingdom and I will show you what to desire. You can't trust all matters of the heart and what it says. One minute it is telling you to leave then the next you're willing to sleep in his bed, double minded in all your ways. Are you ready to be made whole and end this cycle? Please tell me. Do you truly want to be made free? I want you to be free. Free to love, free to dance, free to choose me with your whole heart. Allow peace to be your portion because what's true and meant for you will last THROUGH THE TEST OF TIME. So don't settle for any more potential. No more begging, asking for commitments FOR THE NEXT ONE, JUST do it my way, it's only a matter of time. He's coming!

*I*t Depends

Torn in between the two, as
if I should stay or go.

I guess you left me no options,
but why am I bothered and
undecided?

A double-minded man
is unstable in all his ways. Lord,
help me,
because I feel blinded.

A reprobated mind,
thrown to his devour. In
this hour,
I will not be fooled anymore or a
coward.

What I need the most, Lord, is
your Holy Ghost power.

I got to heal.
Create in me a clean heart
and renew the right spirit in me.

Open my eyes to see that
what's sent by you
must come rooted in you.

It all depends,
should I stay.

or should I let you in, If
this is true.

I NEED ANSWERS; my hope in love
depends on you.

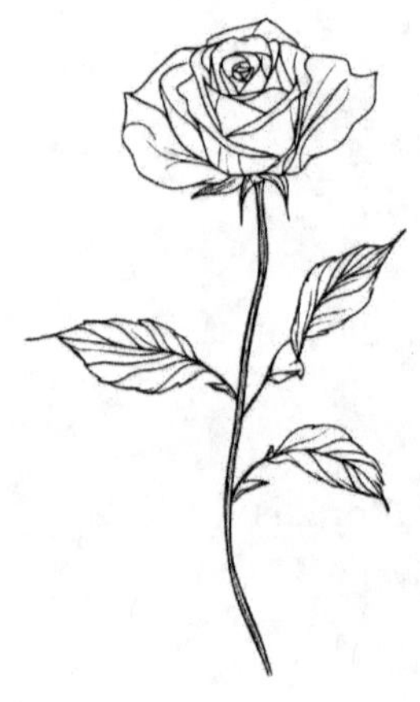

*P*ick Me

I don't want to be picked on, chasing after any type of man that barely gets me. Not to mention, after they get your number, they won't replay back or pay you any attention. I should be offended by the lack thereof. Waiting in hopes that they will stay. I say "hey," cause I'm not chasing a feeling, what a joke you still haven't grown to see your worth. Don't accept the bare minimum, even the comments they leave I should be offended, it's a set up, so get up.
Little do you know they are grooming you, but they claim that its temperature checks with ill intentions. Not to mention. This is just to show them what they can do and get away with you, but it caught you slipping.

No, you don't need that type of attention.
They feeding you crumbs just to hold up space, but they are not willing. Pay attention, I hope you listen. You can't laugh this off anymore, it is uncomfortable. Please don't ignore that feeling.

*L*ove Is Not A Performance

Lord, help me to see myself the way you see me. Show me my worth and how a man should love me.

I'M SO tired of the performance. Show up like this, do that, I'm tired of doing backflips. Can I experience something real? Someone who loves me and sees me. Someone who makes me a part of their world. That's a big deal. I have never experienced this type of love yet. I'm holding onto love because I want it to be real. Is there something that is wrong with me? How come what I want, won't choose me? Why am I skipped over? Is there something that I missed? What happened to my favor?

Please Lord, renew my mind and help me to see me. I'm trying hard not to fight this.

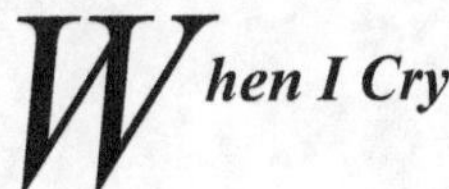

When I Cry

When I cry, you cry.
Lord, you hear me through the night.

Please hold me tight and hide me.
Take the pain away from me.
I'm tryna keep it together,
but these feelings keep choking me in the night.

It's coming up, I'm coming out, washed and made
clean. It's the glory that you send late at night. It
heals me.

It's good to know that I'm seen. While

I wait and be still, I just pray.
Like can I skip past this old thing that's weighing
heavy and just get to the good part of things?

On the next side, the best side, where
it's free and clear.

Thank you, Lord, for washing the dirt off me, So,
I can breathe in peace.

I got this feeling that when I cry, you cry, we cry.
Thank you Lord for always listening to me.

*D*isappearing Act

HOW COULD the one I gave my heart to, share my dreams with, confess the words I love you, yet their actions say otherwise? Like do you even like me? Why haven't you called me? The feeling of begging for attention later turned into bitter resentment. How come they can't see that it's me? It sucks I couldn't even notice your presence since you were so distant, I barely even missed it. This feeling creates a void of loneliness and distance even while you are with them. The void of you not really knowing me. You never saw me for who I am. Moments and opportunities missed, yet after a while I got used to it. This void created an emptiness that I hid with such pride. I realised it was pride all along, because I didn't think anything was wrong with me, so what's wrong? It's me you SEE. I didn't want to face myself and when the quietness got louder, I began to weep.

I cried to be seen, I
cried to be held, I
cried for me.

I cried because things felt so hard just to complete, yet I felt like I couldn't show it. I had to show up my best. I had to show up, but I couldn't hold myself together.

So, that night, I gave myself permission to feel and be seen. I gave myself permission to cry.

That night I cried for me.
I cried so that God would hear me and come see me.
That night, I cried and I cried until I cried myself to sleep.

I Ain't Mad At Cha

I hate seeing you go,
but I understand why you must
leave.

I ain't mad at cha.
I trust God,
so I get it respectfully.

He brings me peace. I
now have clarity.

Friends come
and friends go,
even some loved ones leave.

The silence is loud.
it's a shift I see

So I'm not mad at cha.
In due time,
I will understand,
because I know,
that in all things,
that God sees.

He sees my cries; he
sees you and me.

He sees the things
that were said
behind my back

that I cannot see.

It's okay.
I see.

No lost love
between you and
me.

I release you into the
freedom of my
forgiveness.

I ain't mad at cha
Trust me.

AFFLICTION SCRIPTURES

CORINTHIANS 12:9–10 (NIV)

But he said to me, "My grace is sufficient for you, for my power is made perfect in weakness."

Therefore I will boast all the more gladly about my weaknesses, so that Christ's power may rest on me.

That is why, for Christ's sake, I delight in weaknesses, in insults, in hardships, in persecutions, in difficulties.

For when I am weak, then I am strong.

JAMES 1:2–4 (NIV)

Consider it pure joy, my brothers and sisters, whenever you face trials of many kinds,

because you know that the testing of your faith produces perseverance.

Let perseverance finish its work so that you may be mature and complete, not lacking anything.

1 PETER 5:7 (NIV)

Cast all your anxiety on him because he cares for you.

PSALM 46:1 (NIV)

God is our refuge and strength, an ever-present help in trouble.

*A*FFLICTION SCRIPTURES

ACTS 16:25 (NIV)

About midnight Paul and Silas were praying and singing hymns to God, and the other prisoners were listening to them.

ROMANS 5:3–5 (NIV)

Not only so, but we also glory in our sufferings, because we know that suffering produces perseverance; perseverance, character; and character, hope.
And hope does not put us to shame, because God's love has been poured out into our hearts through the Holy Spirit, who has been given to us.

PSALM 62:8 (NIV)

Trust in him at all times, you people; pour out your hearts to him, for God is our refuge.

LAMENTATIONS 3:22–23 (NIV)

Because of the Lord's great love we are not consumed, for his compassions never fail. They are new every morning; great is you r faithfulness.

*Q*UESTIONS

1. What is this affliction teaching me about my faith and trust in God?

2. How do I usually respond to hardship, fear, anger, patience, or hope and how might God be shaping that response?

3. What part of this struggle feels hardest to surrender to God? Have I noticed moments of God's presence, comfort, or provision in the middle of my pain?

____

____

____

____

____

____

____

____

____

____

____

____

____

____

____

Chapter 2

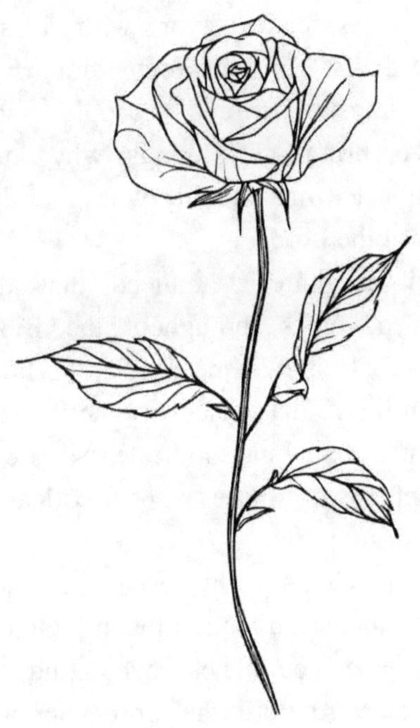

FAVOR

Finding favor in God's sight is something many of us desire. We often associate favor with blessings, rewards, access, and open doors. Yet, for a long time, I wondered why some of the most favored people still experienced suffering. If favor brings good things, why does hardship still exist? This question led me to study what it truly means to find favor in the sight of the Lord.

As I studied Scripture, I noticed that the word favor appears hundreds of times throughout the Bible. In Strong's Concordance, the Hebrew meaning of favor is closely connected to humility. That discovery shifted my perspective. What if favor is not something God releases after we arrive, but something He entrusts to those who first learn how to walk humbly?

Finding favor in God's sight reveals the posture of one's heart. It requires submission and allowing God to search you, refine you, and shape you. Those who find favor are those who humble themselves before the Lord. Scripture reminds us to "humble yourself before the Lord," because humility positions us to be seen by God in the way we are asking to be seen.

If we are praying for God to notice us, to meet our needs, or to visit us in a special way, we must first be willing to humble ourselves before Him. Favor cannot be found apart from humility. You cannot seek God's sight while resisting surrender.

Ruth understood this posture when she said:

"Let me find favor in your sight, my lord, for you have comforted me and spoken kindly to your servant, though I do not belong to your people." *(Ruth 2:13)*

Finding favor is not performance driven. It is not about doing the right things so that God responds in return. God is not a genie, and favor is not a reward system or a magic formula. God desires relationships. And out of relationships flows obedience, reverence, and a genuine desire to please Him. When you love the Lord, your life begins to reflect that love. Scripture reminds us: "Do you not know that your body is the temple of the Holy Spirit?" *(1 Corinthians 6:19)*

Living a life that honors God presenting your body, heart, and choices as pure is pleasing to Him. Not because of work, but because of intimacy.

Finding favor with the Lord also means that He is pleased with you. This does not mean striving or working to earn His approval. Moses experienced this kind of favor when the Lord said: *"I will do the very thing you have asked, because I am pleased with you and I know you by name." (Exodus 33:17)* Because of that favor, Moses asked boldly: "Now show me your glory." *(Exodus 33:18)*

And the Lord responded: *"I will cause all my goodness to pass in front of you, and I will proclaim my name, the Lord, in your presence. I will have mercy on whom I will have mercy, and I will have compassion on whom I will have compassion. "(Exodus33:19)* Favor flows from intimacy. Humility makes room for relationship, and relationship opens the door to seeing God more clearly with Eyes Wide Open.

As you read this chapter and the poems that follow, understand this: favor does not always feel good. Some things will require you to let go. Some of the poems in this chapter reflect experiences of love, loss, surrender, and refinement. They reveal the cost of being seen by God and the process of becoming who He is calling you to be. Favor will cost you something.

Read this chapter with patience and honesty. Allow the words and poems to sit with you. Do not rush to find yourself in them, let God reveal what needs to be seen. Favor is not always comfortable, but it is always purposeful.

Read with humility.
Read with openness.
Read with your Eyes Wide Open.

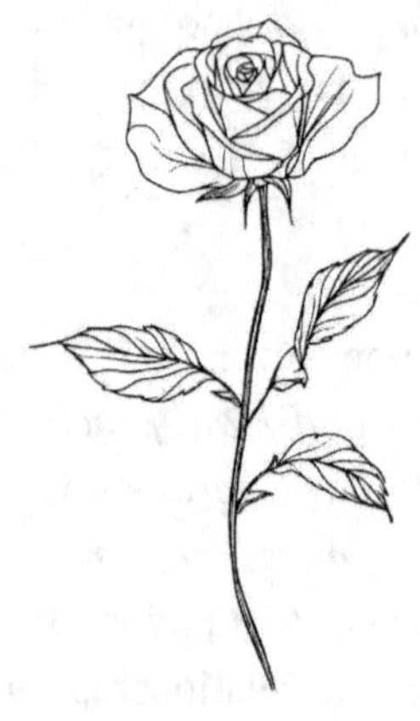

Goodness Favor

Goodness and faithfulness
stored up
just for me and you.

Only a few understand it.
They understand
that God's love for them is
not wrapped
in a performance.

God's goodness
they won't take for granted.

People ask and wonder,
how this could be?

If God loves you so much,
why the uncertainty? Why,
and how,
could bad things
happen to me?

What they don't see
is God still working things
out for their good.

It doesn't matter
if you don't know it. He's
God.

He's good And He's
true.

Is this a God
who gives generously
to his children? Yes,
that can be you.

What you see is favor
flowing abundantly.

Unmerited favor,
blessing on blessing,
and many open doors,
working
in one man's life.

This goodness could
be yours.

Only if you have faith
and never forget that
he that began a good
work in you will
complete it until
performance.

This is the evidence
laid up

for all who love,
wait, and trust in the
Lord.

*L*ook Away

SOME THINGS YOU MUST ERASE, delete, and remove from your path. Clear out the history, get rid of any stains, or old memories of once was. Cut off the oxygen and detach from the attachments of the past. Don't look back, double back, or try to spin the block. What if the closure is looking away?

IT'S easy to let someone back in when there's a crack in the door. Often, we go back to old things because we weren't finished yet, or simply not sure. Too afraid of the future, mistakes, mishaps and disappointments. I get it, it can be hard to believe what we cannot see. Yet, still look away and continue to move forward. Be in a place of expectation that your greatest blessing is waiting for you on the other side of the door.

*K*nock

<u>K</u>now that you are loved *(1 John 4:9-11)*
<u>N</u>ow surely, I will answer *(Jeremiah 15:11)*
<u>O</u>bserve my ways *(Proverbs 23:26)*
<u>C</u>ome to me if you are weary *(Matthew 11:28-29)*
<u>K</u>now that I am God *(Psalm 46:10)*

<u>K</u>now that you are my beloved *(John 13:35)*
<u>N</u>ow faith is the evidence of things hoped for and the assurance
about what we do not see *(Hebrews 11:1)*
<u>O</u>ut of your belly shall flow rivers of living water *(John 7:38)* <u>C</u>ome to me all who are weary and heavy *(Matthew 11:28-29)* <u>K</u>now that I called you and set you apart *(Psalm 4:3)*

<u>K</u>now my voice *(John 10:27-28)*
<u>N</u>ow stir up the gift *(2 Timothy 1:6)*
<u>O</u>n this rock I will build my church *(Matthew 16:18)*
<u>C</u>ount it all joy when trails arise *(James 1:2-4)*
<u>K</u>now that I am the God who sees *(Isaiah 26:3)*

It's Possible

It is so,
yes, it is true.

Having the
impossible can
happen to you.

Exceeding,
abundantly, above
all
is what it will be
for you.

It is possible, yes,
it is possible,
and it is very true.

It is possible
that it will turn
in your favor.

Blessings and
abundance can
happen
for you.

It is raining,
sounds of heavy rain.

Your blessing is
on its way

to you.

Believe the possible,
because it is possible.

You are possible. it
will be a miracle for
you.

Rediscovering You

I see how you made
me, how you formed
me in my mother's
womb.

You, my God, have
chosen me.

Before I had
answered the call
you gave me, you
heard me.

That is when I
started to

rediscover who you
are,
not what my mother
had told me.

I rediscovered
what you have given me.

You gave me favor. You
gave me a new life.

You gave me new
meaning to reach my
destiny.

You gave a
reason to love,
to dance,
and to worship
you, with my
whole heart.

I then
rediscovered the
real me.

I discovered
who I am truly
at heart.

I, your daughter, have
rediscovered your love
for me.

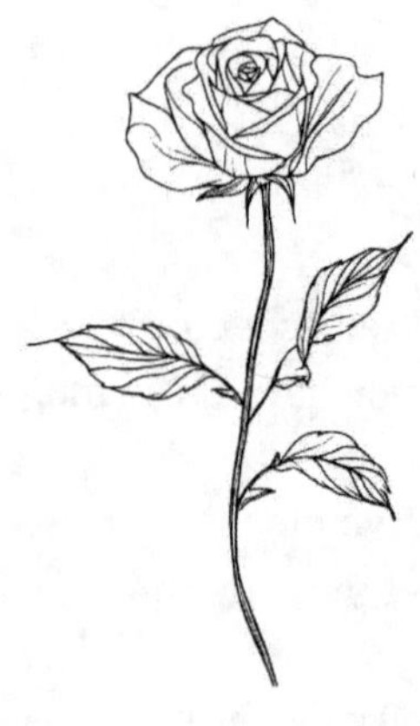

Grow

If you had to grow up without a father, role model or male figure in your life, just know that God hears your silent cry. He's raising you up now, he will be a father to the fatherless, let him call you, his son. He's giving you a new name, new identity and vision of yourself so take the blinders of your eyes so you can see. He's giving you a garment of praise for the spirit of heavniess. He's giving you fresh oil for the calling on your life. He's leading you and walking you through open doors. In Him, you're enough, you're capable, and ambitious. You are royalty, you are a leader sent by a King, that's why you're so strong. Be brave in your walk and every move you make. Keep going, keep pushing, keep working and building your foundation to be a better you. You're destined for greatness. Grow in maturity of your faith. This time you will know who you are. In this season you will find favor with God and man.

F*lower Print*

I SEE YOU AS A FLOWER.

You touch souls with every
smile that you
bring.

Your essence is beautiful You
have a heart
so pure.

It's the joy that
you bring.

I see why people stop
and stare,
that's how valuable you are.

You can light up any
room
and fill people's souls
with love.

That's your superpower. That's
your favor.

You are
the light
of the world.

Please don't hesitate
to leave your flower prints
on the world,
baby girl.

Be authentically you.

You are
one out of one.

This is why
you cannot hide nor
run
from the call
I have placed on you.

I created you
and fashioned you as
such.

You are a rose,
just like the rose
that grew from the concrete
with every plea,
in places,
speaks to the radiance you
have inside of you.

The thorns are there,
but they were never meant
to hurt you.

They were for
pruning,
for you to bear
more fruit.

So, bloom
and step into the new.

Receive the blessings
that I have
in store
for you.

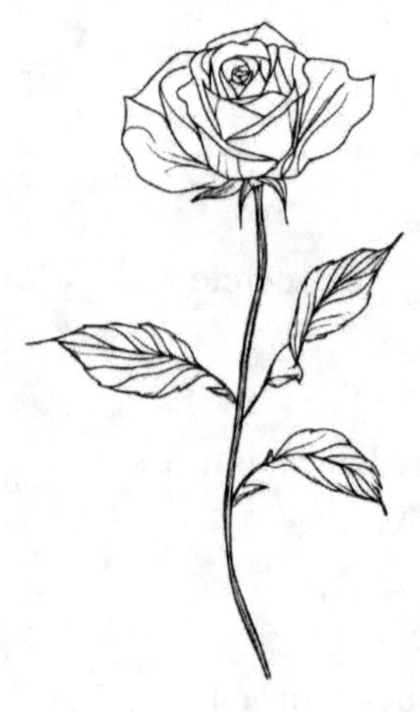

*S*oft Places

Pay attention to your body and what it needs. Moments of rest where you can simply just breathe. Create a safe environment where you can practice being gentle to yourself. Seek love, healing, or any blessings, of the good things you want to see. Process every emotion in prayer and express your feelings to God. Release tears give yourself time to slow down. Create a soft place, and a safe place where you're free to be you.

*S*uddenly

Any minute now is all I can say.
That God is knocking at your door; the answers are flowing
your way. Any minute now, you could walk into your
blessings, any minute now, you can meet the love of your
life. Any minute now, your blessing can arrive. Attach your
faith to this, suddenly.

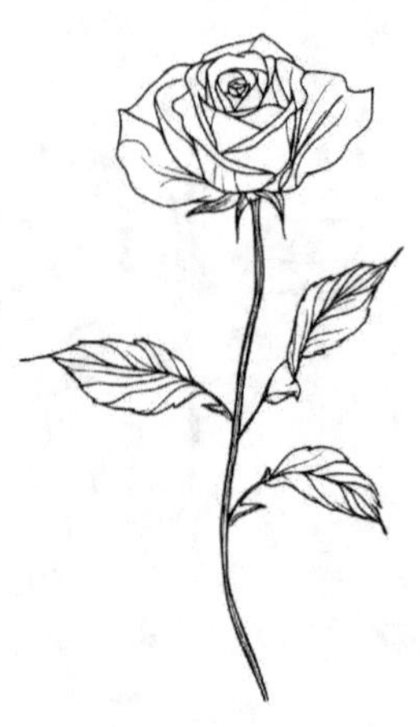

*O*ne In A Million

This love is a one-in- a- million
kind of love.

I'm talking about
the love of a lifetime.

It's so divine.
It gets so much better
over time,
and this love is mine.

A love that's rooted in
spirit
and truth.

So divinely orchestrated by the
Lord.
You are one of a kind.

This is a one- in-a-million, love
of a lifetime
thing.

A love that can stand the
test of time.

This love is holy
and pure.

There is safety in
your comfort and
in your presence,
I am sure.

That it is me you
have been
looking for.

I know you, and
you see me.

This kinda love
brings me
so much joy.

*B*athroom Wall

1. Don't force it
2. If it's meant for you, it will be there
3. Smile, life can be worse
4. Be thankful
5. It's okay if you make mistakes
6. It's already yours
7. Love hard, alway
8. Try something new
9. Pray about everything
10. Just be you

*F*AVOR SCRIPTURES

1 SAMUEL 1:18 And she said, let thine handmaid find grace in thy sight. So, the woman went her way, and did eat, and her countenance was no more sad.

GENESIS 6:8 "But NOAH found grace in the eyes of the LORD.

GENESIS 18:3 "AND SAID, My Lord, if now I have found favor in thy sight, pass not away, I pray thee, from thy servant:

GENESIS 19:19 "BEHOLD NOW, thy servant hath found grace in thy sight, and thou hast magnified thy mercy, which thou hast shewed unto me in saving my life.

FAVOR SCRIPTURES

EXODUS 33:35 "Yet you have said, I know you by name, and you have also found favor in my sight. Now therefore, If I have found favor in your sight

MATTHEW 6:22 "The eye is the lamp of the body. If your eyes are healthy, your whole body will be full of light"

LUKE 10:23 "Then he turned to his disciples and said privately, "Blessed are the eyes that see what you see"

LUKE 24:31 "Then their eyes were opened, and they recognized him, and he disappeared from their sight

*Q*UESTIONS

1. Where, in my life have, I clearly seen God's favor?

2. What role do faith, humility, and obedience play in experiencing God's favor?

3. How can I live so that God's favor blesses others through me?

4. Do I recognize that God's favor is a gift of grace and not something I earn?

____
____
____
____
____
____
____
____
____
____
____
____
____
____

Chapter 3

3

QUESTIONS

God sees every question we bring before Him, but the cost of seeing those answers comes with a greater level of responsibility. When revelation comes, so does accountability. What God reveals, He also expects us to steward.

We all have questions for God, questions we long to have answered. I believe these questions are good because they draw us closer to Him. They cause us to seek God for guidance, direction, and instruction. Questions invite intimacy.

> "Lord, I'm afraid, afraid I may fail. I
> feel like a failure sometimes.
> What if I over shared this too soon?"

What feels hardest, though, is not asking the questions, it's waiting for God to answer them. Waiting requires stillness. It requires trust. It means being okay with when God responds and how He chooses to move. Waiting stretches our faith.

Questions are necessary because God does not want us to walk blindly or live without understanding. He desires that we seek Him, not just for answers, but for relationships. However, once God responds, that's when the real work begins.

Once you are free and delivered, you must maintain it. Every new level requires a deeper level of surrender, discipline, and dependence on the power of the Holy Spirit to lead and guide you in your faith walk.

Jesus demonstrated this when He healed the blind man. He told him to,"Go, wash in the Pool of Siloam" *(John 9:7 NIV)*. The word Siloam means "sent." The man obeyed, he went, washed, and came home seeing.

What stands out to me is that this miracle required the blind man's participation. He had to believe he was healed before he could see. He had to move in faith and do the work of washing his eyes. Healing didn't come without obedience.

Scripture reminds us, "Draw near to God, and He will draw near to you" *(James 4:8)*. God has already sent His Word. It is available to us to cleanse, to heal, and to set us free. Maybe the work God is asking of you is to wash the dirt from your eyes so you can truly see.

Questions are necessary because God desires a relationship with you. As you draw closer to Him, be ready to wash. Be willing to rinse your eyes, release what once clouded your vision, and see clearly with your *Eyes Wide Open*.

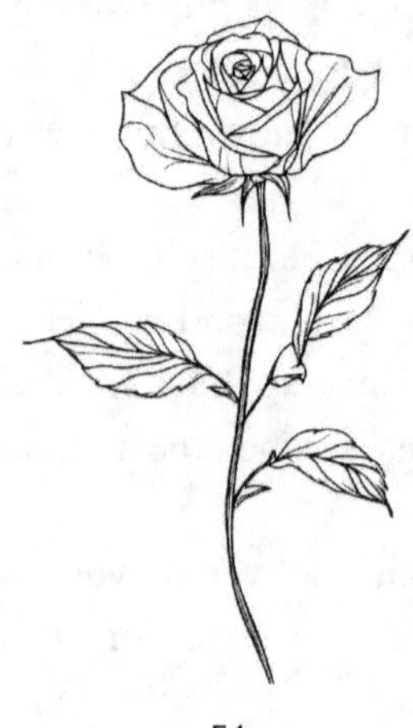

QUESTIONS

Dear Lord,

I am ready. I feel that I am ready now to see. I'm ready to see the truth in all things, even if that truth hurts me. I'm ready to change now.

Read this chapter slowly. Pause when something challenges you. Reflect when a Scripture or poem resonates. Ask yourself: Where do I need to obey? Where do I need to wash the dirt from my eyes so I can truly see?

This chapter is an invitation not just to understand God's answers, but to participate in them. Approach it with humility, openness, and a willingness to act. Your faith is strengthened not only in knowing, but in doing.

Read with humility.
Read with openness.
Read with your eyes wide open.

*G*ames Being Played

WHAT TYPE of games are there being played? How's it going down? You give your toughest battles to your soldiers. You know, like the generals, who are ready, trained and equipped. Yet, I just keep finding myself getting whipped. I'm hit, trying my hardest to get back up and not quit. I didn't forget what you said. You said, "I can do all things through Christ who strengthens me *(Philippians 4:13)*." So, here's my lament.

Father, strengthen me. Help me, so I can go back and get my brother. Keep me from falling back into my old ways. Keep my mind far from sin. Keep my mind on your perfect peace. Lord, you said your sheep know your voice, now Father hear my cry. Send me favor and good speed, show me your grace please don't turn away from me. I see the weapons of my warfare, help me take down the strong man in my life. I have no choice but to go to the battlefield. So which arsenal should I use? Is it praise? Sacrifice? Or worship? What do you need me to do? Which tool should I use? For the pulling down of strong holds in my life. Train me up, Lord, and make me a ready vessel. Lord, I'm trying to get it right. Make me an offering, make me whatever you need me to be. Make me the person who seeks you and delights in your ways. Lord, make me open, give me sight to see. Lord, make me ready to fight with you in war. See my needs and hear my heart's cry, please Lord it's me, no more games being played. I'm tired of being left ignored.

Waiting

Waiting on this, and
waiting on that.

People love to say,
" waiting takes time", but
what if waiting
really takes God?

Can you ask yourself,
are you truly waiting,
or are you waiting, but
complaining?

Do you have enough
faith to wait for it
patiently?

What is your heart
producing? Can you trust
that
it's coming?

Can you rest in uncertainty even
when you can't see anything?

Is this truly waiting?
And how well can you wait?
What does it take?
Do you have endurance?

I pray God increases your faith.

While you wait,
his time
be certain
and settled in your spirit
that everything is secure

You're not gonna guess or
doubt.
You will trust in
the Lord.

Be sure,
that all things are working
for you.

The Lord is not a man that
He will lie to.
He is sure,
and certain about you.

He has you,
and everything you need in
His hands.

He is concerned about you,
but He is watching
how you wait.

So, wait on the Lord and
be of good courage.

Your strength will
be renewed.

So wait well
this time.

The matter is
sorted, for sure.

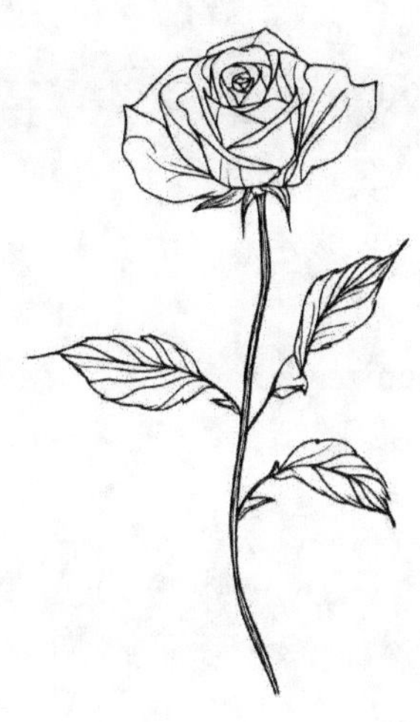

*S**leep Outside***

Have you ever slept
outside in the cold?

I can't imagine how
that would be.

To lose the things you
love, your comfort,
your home, only
to beg
for someone to see.

Someone to recognize you
for who you are,
and not your
shortcomings or
circumstances
they perceive.

If you ever glimpse
someone sleeping outside
in the cold, please give
them this
from me?

Some bread to eat,
water to drink, and
money
to cover any fees.

If you sow these
deeds to someone
who sleeps outside in
the cold,
just know
you also
are feeding me.

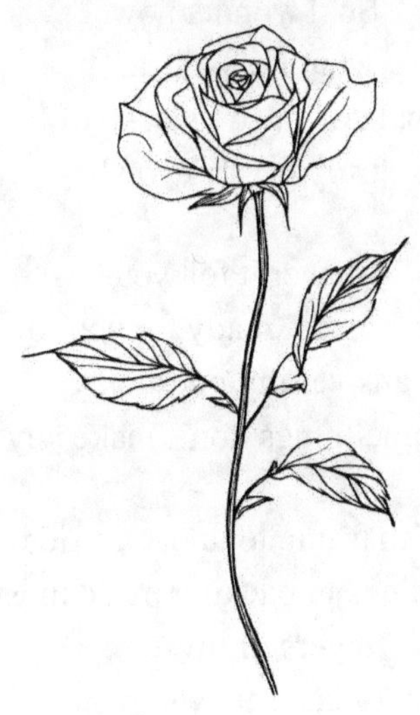

What Do I Have to Lose?

What do I have to lose, if I
put my trust in you?
I'm tired of being confused.

Jumping from place-to-place,
feeling like,
what else do I have to do?

So, I wonder now,
what I must lose?
What do I need to let go of to
truly trust in you?

I haven't felt you.
I'm steady, ready for you to
answer my questions,
because some things don't make any sense.

It's like I'm trying to unpack a riddle, but
the riddle is unpacking me, exposing
layers of myself,
just so that I can see what you can see.

I keep praying that my prayers are hitting heaven
and that you hear me.
I know you will see me.

So, I ask again,
what more is

required of me?

What do you want me to
do? Open my eyes to
see you,
Lord, my eyes are
focused this time on
you.

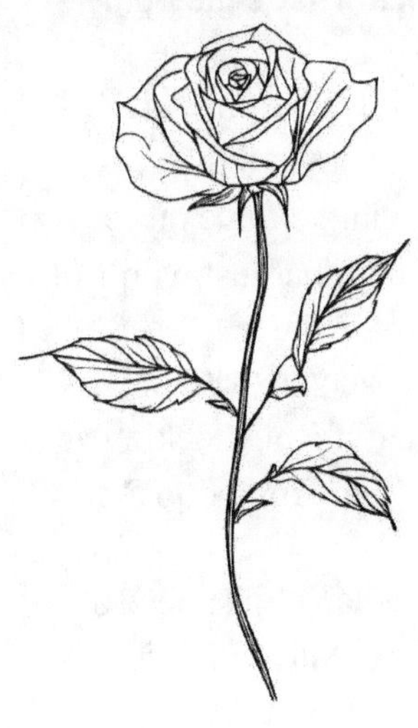

Finish It

Dear Lord,
can you help me finish it?

I don't want to keep
starting something new to
only come up short.

Cause if that's the case,
then what's the point?

Steadily moving
here and there,
trying to force pieces
together that just won't fit.

Maybe that's it.
What if I'm knocking at
the wrong door?

Perhaps I just need a
change, Maybe it's just the
weather.

Am I heading in the right
way?

What do you want me to do?
I feel like it's harder

to get next to you.

Draw me close to
you.

Right now,
I just want to stay here
and lay
at your feet.

Help me, Lord, to
trust you more.

I want to find
rest in you.

Lord, please give me
direction. Give me
wisdom and
understanding.

Lord, please help me
to see this through.
I want the blessing.

*O*ld Enough

I ALWAYS HAD questions about everything when I was young, and I see why. I wanted to grow so much and have my own, but now I sit and wish time could slow down. It's funny how things change, always tryna speed up the time not realising that great things take time. You must be patient and wait. So now, I slow down and take my time to find my own pace. I see that I'm my own goals, what's there to compare? I need my place and my space so I can create. In due time, they say, "God bless the kid who has its own," and I know why. Now that I'm old enough, I stay to myself, free myself from all the past trauma to see who I really am. I'm free to be all of myself, not caring what nobody has to say, I'm doing me. Who's asking now? What's your truth? What's your worth? Have you been searching for answers? What's your outlet? Inspiration? I SEE YOU accomplished so much. Keep going, building from scratch takes courage. I'm old enough to know that I couldn't have gotten to where I'm at without any help, my biggest support system cheering me on. They paved the way for me, and for that, I'm old enough to pay my deepest respect to those before me. This walk isn't easy.

*S**afe or Sorry?***

PAY ATTENTION, do they make you feel safe or sorry? This can save you the heartbreak. What are you able to pick up? Look beyond what the eyes can see. What does the fruit say? Do they bring joy, peace, or love in any way? Yea, I'm judging, be judgy and inspect the fruit just as if it was yours to eat. Let's run it back without making any choices, is it safe or sorry? Who is the person? Do they leave you feeling confused in your mind? Left constantly wondering who you are to them? How does your body respond? Are you anxious? nervous? jittery with them? Perhaps all these feelings you have are new and you can't make up in your head what is best. I get it, you want to be safe, not sorry. Think about these words and reset.

The blessing makes a man rich and adds no sorrow *(Proverbs 10:22)*. Please check the fruit. Then you will quickly detect if it's safe or sorry.

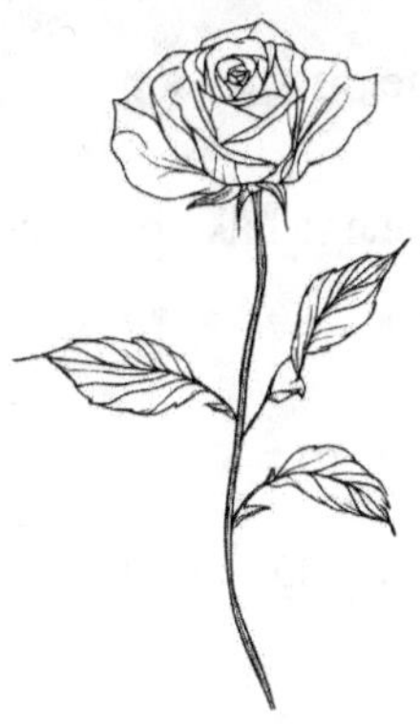

Feeling Afraid?

Lord, I'm afraid. I'm afraid I may
fail. I feel like a failure sometimes.
What if I over-shared this too soon?

People are watching me. Some
take notice and applaud,
while others simply don't like me.

So why me?
What's the hold up? People
tryna fight me?

Nothing feels like it's on the move.

Lord, send me Your word today, and
tell me what You want me to do.
What should I read and listen to?

I'm public now.
Did I step out of the pit too soon?

I don't want everyone to talk about me
while I hear it
and not listen to You.

Listen.
Fear is steadily knocking,

but I won't listen.

This time,
I will pay attention.
This time,
I'm ready to listen.

I'm done being afraid.
I want to grow up
and get out of my
feelings.

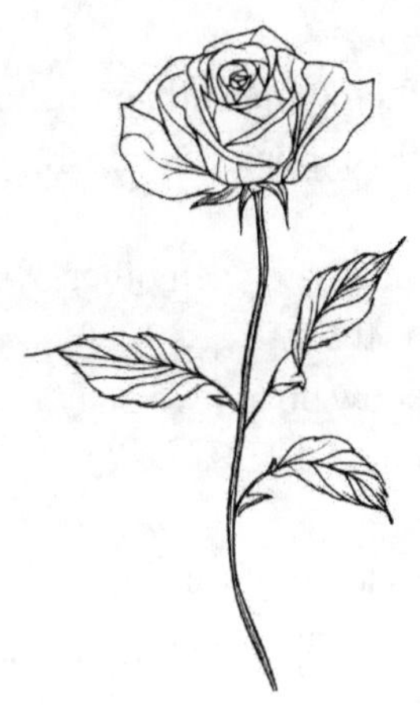

*I*ntimacy

How do you measure intimacy?
True intimacy will always get put to
the test.

We measure intimacy by being seen. I
start first,
and you go next.
We listen,
and we don't judge

This intimacy I give you can
you see it?
Intimacy is being opened and naked.
Can you fully expose your flesh?

We give intimacy to each other by
honoring our truth,
by how we show up to love and
trust each other.

Can you measure your intimacy?
What does your heart say?

Be vulnerable,
and willing to flow with the
connection and create intimacy at its
best.

Bear Witness

Do you want the truth? No
lies, well here it is.

Jesus has been looking for someone to bear witness to who He
is. Now tell me the truth, are you truthful? Are
you even kind?

Are you patient in the things that you do? What

you post on social media, is it true?
Do you show honesty about the way you live and the things
you do? Taking on false identities, character flaws, masking
these personality traits, like it's really you? Is it real?

Lights off, cameras off now, is it real?
What do you see when you look at yourself in the mirror?
Do you know the real you?
Who are you when you go back to the crib, when no one is
watching?
Is it real? or is it for show?
Masking yourself thinking no one will know.

I pray that you will take off the mask of what you think you
know. I pray the Holy Spirit will show a side of you that you
never thought to know.
Can this be so?

He said, "behold I will do a new thing," so that it is not
strange. When our Heavenly Father, who created you, shows
you, you will start to show.
This time, everyone will know that the Lord has met you.
This is the confidence you can boast in, and yea ya skin
gonna glow.

It's time to grow.
He makes things beautiful in His perfect timing, and
you are the evidence of His masterpiece.

I'm a living witness to this, all the testimony is starting to
show. It's the glory He gave me,
and I give it back to Him so that everyone will know.

If you're ever wondering, how can we bear witness to Christ
with our actions?
What do I say, you may be thinking, "I don't know."

Show them love by listening and being encouraged can be a
start. God's faithfulness and loyalty I hope everyone
can see.
He paid it all, simply for you and me.

I HOPE this encourages you to always spread love and
good news. Bear witness to Christ's love and His actions
by showing others all what He has done for you.

QUESTIONS SCRIPTURES

PSALM 13:1 (NIV)

How long, Lord? Will you forget me
forever? How long will you hide your face
from me?

JEREMIAH 12:1 (NIV)

You are always righteous, Lord, when I bring a case
before you. Yet, I would speak with you about your
justice: Why
does the way of the wicked prosper? Why do all the
faithless live at ease?

HABAKKUK 2:3 (NIV)

For the revelation awaits an appointed time; it
speaks of the end and will not prove false. Though
it linger, wait for it;
it will certainly come and will not delay.

*Q*UESTIONS SCRIPTURES

Isaiah 55:8–9 (NIV)

"For my thoughts are not your thoughts,

neither are your ways my ways," declares the Lord. "As the heavens are higher than the earth, so are my ways higher than your ways and my thoughts than your thoughts."

PROVERBS 3:5–6 (NIV)

Trust in the Lord with all your heart
and lean not on your own understanding; in all your ways submit to him, and he will make your paths straight.

PSALM 77:11–12 (NIV)

I will remember the deeds of the Lord; yes, I will remember your miracles of long ago. I will consider all your works and meditate on all your mighty deeds.

Questions

1.What is the deepest question or doubt I am carrying, and how honestly can I bring it to God?

2.How might God be inviting me to trust Him even when I don't understand His timing?

3.What can I learn about myself, my faith, and my relationship with God through my questions?

4.Are there recurring questions or frustrations I keep asking God?What might He be teaching me

____
____
____
____
____
____
____
____
____
____
____
____
____
____

Chapter 4

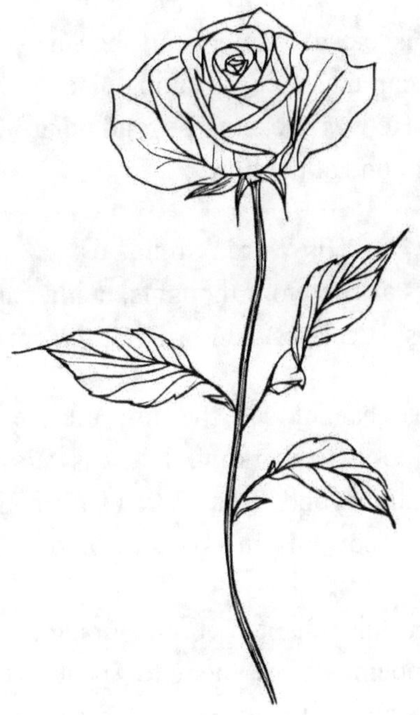

4

ANSWERS

God answers prayer.

This chapter is close to my heart because, as I wrote these words, I could hear the Lord speaking. He wasn't just speaking to my situation, He was speaking beyond what I could see, beyond what I even understood at the time.

His Word reminds us:
"For my thoughts are not your thoughts, neither are your ways my ways," declares the Lord. *(Isaiah 55:8-9)*

Even when we cannot see the full picture, even when our questions remain, God is working. His answers, His timing, and His plans are far beyond what we can imagine. Sometimes, the work of faith is not only in asking questions, but in trusting the One who already knows.

As you finish this chapter, I encourage you to pause and reflect on each poem. Allow them to speak into your situation. Some of these poems will also reveal where you are hiding. God doesn't want us to sit on our gifts and not use them. These poems will put a mirror to the truth. As God speaks, he also affirms. Some of these poems will affirm that He did hear you and He sees you. As you read this chapter, think about what God has been showing you through your questions. Where have you been called to act in faith? And what is He teaching you about patience, surrender, and trust in His perfect plan?

Remember: seeing clearly, walking boldly, and living with

Eyes Wide Open means trusting the One who sees it all, even when you cannot. He knows your heart, He knows your path, and He is faithful to answer in His perfect timing. Let this chapter remind you: God answers prayers. Not always in the way we expect, not always on our timeline, but always according to His will, His purpose, and His plan he has for us.

Read with humility.
Read with openness.
Read with your Eyes Wide Open.

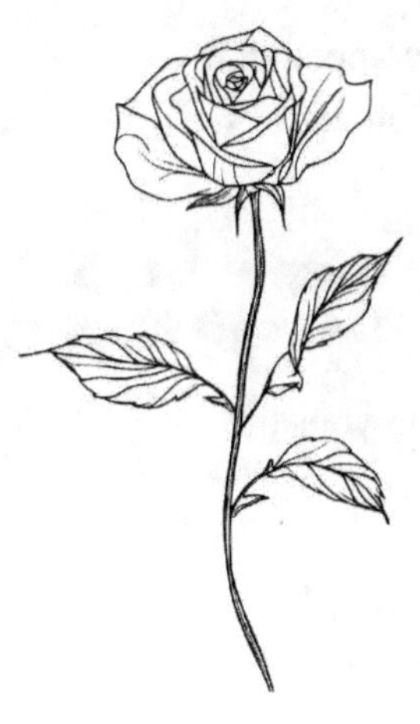

When I See You

When I see you,
I don't see where you're at, I
see where you're going.

When I see you,
I look past your faults.
As a matter of fact,
I don't even see them

When I see you,
I see you for who I
called you to be.

When I see you,
I see you wrapped in my
love and clothed in
goodness
and mercy.

When I see you,
I see light in your life
and hope that lives in me.

When I see you, I
see purpose and
prosperity.

When I see you,
I'm reminded of the
reflection and image of me

that you carry.

When I see you,
I see an overcomer
who is more than a
conqueror.

When I see you, I
see excellence and
power.

I see you as the head
and not the tail.
I see you as the
lender and not the
borrower.

When I see you, I
see victory, and a
champion.

When I see you,
I see my son whom
I love dearly.

When I stop
to take notice of you,
it's like I see you
for the first time all
over again.

When I see you just
know
that I am very
pleased.

F*rontin'*

You think no one sees you, but I do.
You can't hide who you are; you should stop frontin', because
you are not fouling anybody but yourself. I see you and I know
who you are. You can't hide anymore so come out from among
them.
Be ye holy because I am holy; I'm just saying you gotta stop
frontin'. It's more in you than the bare minimum you have
been giving. So, stop frontin'. No more sitting on the gift I gave
you. Now is the time to rise and be everything I called you to.
Play time is over. I'm only telling you this so you can stop
frontin'.

*D*on't Fold

I'M GROUNDING you right here and now at this moment, so don't fold. Right here you don't have to guess how sure I am about you. I'm rewriting the script for you. So, clock it. Double up and focus on the promise. Open your eyes to me, and I will be your rearguard in this season. Trust me, this is a process. I'm here to help and hold your hand. So don't fold. Don't stop once you pass go, keep pressing. Align yourself to the assignment, and I'll take command. You are now in the right alignment. So, don't fold, don't punk out before the promise. The enemy wants you to quit. You must press forward towards the mark, for this is your high calling. You will lay hold of the promise, I got you, don't fold.

Just Stop

Stop trying
to always make sense of
everything.

You won't always be
given the instructions
up front.

This time,
you must wait.

This is the weight of
the wait.

Rest in it.
This will increase your
faith.

Just stop,
Stop and remember
the last thing
I shared with you and
told you to do.

A lot of your struggles
and hold ups
are because of you.

You kept on quitting,
Don't you know the
enemy is out
to sift you as wheat?

Hang in there. I'm
sending you the
Helper.

This time,
you will not get
weary of doing well,
I will renew your
strength.

Do you believe what
I told you the first
time?

To rest
and abide in me, I
have everything
you need.

Seek first
the kingdom of God,
and all his
righteousness will be
added
to you.

Just stop and put your
faith in me,

and know that I am the
good Shepard.

You will lack nothing
with me.

Quickly

BEHOLD I STAND at the door and knock. Will you let me in? Everything that I'm showing you can happen almost instantly. I see you, I notice how you are counting the time and days of your appointed time.

THIS IS why I have come to you now. Surely, all the things I have desired for you to have will come to pass. And yes, it will happen suddenly.

I HOLD time in my hands. The vision that I have given was made for this divine moment.

NOW, I can release the measure of your promise, and surely as you believe in my words what I am getting ready to do will be a new thing. A good thing, if you only can perceive it.

CAN YOU HEAR THE SOUND? You are under an open heaven, and I will pour you out a blessing, where you don't have enough room to receive it.

,

IF ONLY YOU can believe it and see that this is true. Raise the sound of your faith. Surely, I will come to you quickly and I will not hold back on my word. For this measure of glory,

you can be sure of this. You never deny your blessings, so count it all joy!

B*oasting*

WHO HAS STOLEN MY GLORY? Why have you puffed yourself up instead of coming to me? You flex in what I can give and not my heart. Steady boasting, looking to be seen. But, I was the one who stepped in and set you apart and made you free. If you do celebrate anything, boast about me! I am the Lord who makes all crooked paths straight. So, why have you stolen my glory? This gift of freedom wasn't just for you, but so that everyone can see.This is the way and, I am sure. I have given many gifts and talents, and they all come without repentance. This time, humble yourself before me and you will see this time for sure.

Waiting

WAITING on this and waiting on that. People love to say waiting takes time, but what if waiting really takes God? Can you ask yourself, are you truly waiting or are you waiting, but complaining? Do you have enough faith to wait for it patiently? What is your heart producing? Can you trust that it's coming? Can you rest in uncertainty even when you can't see anything? Is this truly waiting? And how well can you wait? What does it take? Do you have endurance? I pray God increases your faith. While you wait, this time be certain and settled in your spirit that everything is secure. You're not gonna guess or doubt. You will trust in the Lord. Be sure, that all things are working for you, the Lord is not a man that He will lie to. He is sure, and certain about you. He has you, and everything you need in His hands, He is concerned about you, but He is watching how you wait. So, wait on the Lord and be of good courage. Your strength will be renewed, so wait well this time. The matter is sorted for sure.

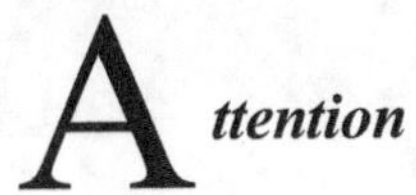*ttention*

Now that I have your attention. I have been here all along
waiting
on you. When you call me, I will listen. I see you.
I need you to draw closer to me at this hour. I need you to hear
from me. Why haven't you ever taken the time to ask me
what have I need of? Or was it always just about meeting your
needs and hearing your feelings? Have you ever tried to listen
to my heart and feel when I hurt?
Did you ask me what you can do to please me?
I do this for you, but did you forget? That you were brought
with a price. I have chosen you and I call you my own. Now
that I have your attention. I can finally show you what your
eyes cannot see. If you are willing to wait, please hear me. I
need your attention.

L et Me

Let me be the reflection that
they see
when they look into your eyes,
they can tell it's me.

Let me be the reflection that
they see.
I want my spirit
to be rooted in you
so you can become like me.

This is the passion.
This is the fire.
I will pour out my spirit to
draw them
to me.

I will be their hope, their
love.
I'll be their protection and
security
when they are not sure.

Let me mend
every broken heart.

Let me use you as an
example so that they
can see my glory from
the start.

If you let me, I
will give you
the desire
you have been
searching for.

I will restore back to you
the years
of wasted time.

I will come quickly and
not delay anything
that's due to you.

I have been searching
and watching
for a pure vessel
like you.

I have set you apart and
aside.
I have your prayer and
request
that you have made
known.

I will show you the
rest, and yes, I heard
your prayer the first
time

I have saved the best
just for you.

So, if you let me,
I will come
and restore the hope
that was stolen from
you.

Let me
into your heart.
Take delight
in my love.
This is the promise.

If you let me, be
ready
to receive
so much more.

W*hite Sheets*

I HAVE PREPARED these sheets for you. You can keep them. I hope you sleep with them at night. Allow these white sheets to bring you rest. I noticed how stressed, tired and worried you were. I looked at you and saw the tears in your eyes flowing. It's something about these white sheets; they won't bring you harm. See, I have prepared these sheets for you, I hope you take them. Allow these sheets to wash your stains away. These white sheets can make blemish and wrinkles brand new. The smell will always linger in the sweet aroma. The feeling will allow you to dwell in my presence, this is heaven. Your sight will indeed be heightened and allow you to see greater things beyond. These white sheets are a gift to you, just as I sent my comforter anytime you may need.

R *eturn*

ARE YOU THIRSTY?

Steady looking for likes and
validation
hoping to be chosen.

That post you made, he
saw it,
but that's not your husband.

No more open doors, and
please,
close your legs.

When will you learn
that love is not
some kind of performance?
HAVEN'T

I not shown you love?

I'm sorry they left you, I'm
sorry he wasn't there,
and daddy couldn't make it to
the rehearsal.

I'm not him.
I'm not anyone
that has left you.

I have always been there
with you,
leading and guiding you
each step of the way.

Your tears,
I see always, and
I can count
the number of them.

I will take care of you. You are
my daughter.

Fearfully and wonderfully,
I have made you.

I have placed everything in
you, so I continue to bloom.

Continue to become
everything I created you to be.

You are my beloved, my
daughter.

You are so precious, and
I am truly pleased with
you.

I love you.

I am forever calling you,
waiting for you to see.

I want you to trust me
more and truly believe
that I have the best
for you.

I would never hurt, you
nor will my words return
to me void.

No more allowing
yourself to think low
and give out discounts.

You are worth so
much more.

I have called you,
my daughter!

You are authentic and
original.
No one can try to compare
or duplicate
the girl that you are. YOU

ARE A DIAMOND.

Don't you dare
shrink back
or hide your face.

You are covered
with my glory.

Abide in me
truly,
this time.

My daughter,
know that you
were that girl.

And I see you.
You make me
proud.

Return to me
and ignore the
crowd.

ANSWERS SCRIPTURES

ISAIAH 55:8–9 (NIV)

"For my thoughts are not your thoughts,
neither are your ways my ways," declares the Lord. "As
the heavens are higher than the earth, so are my ways
higher than your ways and my thoughts than your
thoughts."

PSALM 34:8 (NIV)

Taste and see that the Lord is good; blessed is
the one who takes refuge in him.

Proverbs 19:21 (NIV)

Many are the plans in a person's heart, but it is the
Lord's purpose that prevails.

JAMES 4:3 (NIV)

When you ask, you do not receive, because you ask
with wrong motives, that you may spend what you get on
your pleasures.

ANSWERS SCRIPTURES

PSALM 27:14 (NIV)

Wait for the Lord; be strong and take heart and wait
for the Lord.

LAMENTATIONS 3:25–26 (NIV)

The Lord is good to those whose hope is in
him, to the one who seeks him; it is good to wait
quietly for the salvation of the Lord.

ROMANS 10:17 (NIV)

Consequently, faith comes from hearing the
message, and the message is heard through the word
about Christ.

QUESTIONS

1. How has God's answer revealed His character?

2. How did God's response differ from what I expected, and what can I learn?

3. How did I feel while waiting for the answer, and what did that teach me about patience?

ABOUT THE AUTHOR

A voice of tenderness and truth, Demetria helps believers see themselves clearly. She writes for the one who has ever felt unseen, unheard, or misunderstood. Her mission is to help people see themselves the way God sees them whole, loved, and chosen.

Her creativity is rooted in prayer, ruled by worship, and expressed through storytelling. Her pen carries both softeners and strength, weaving healing into every line. Her writing blends poetry, prayer, and revelation with practical encouragement, and each page feels like a quiet conversation with God.

Demetria's heart is to awaken vision in believers helping them see cleary, live boldly, and walk with purpose. Her words carry the assignment of healing, identity, and spiritual confidence, and her greatest desire is that every reader feels seen, strengthened, and spiritual realigned.

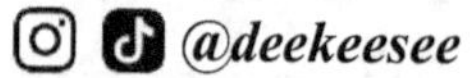